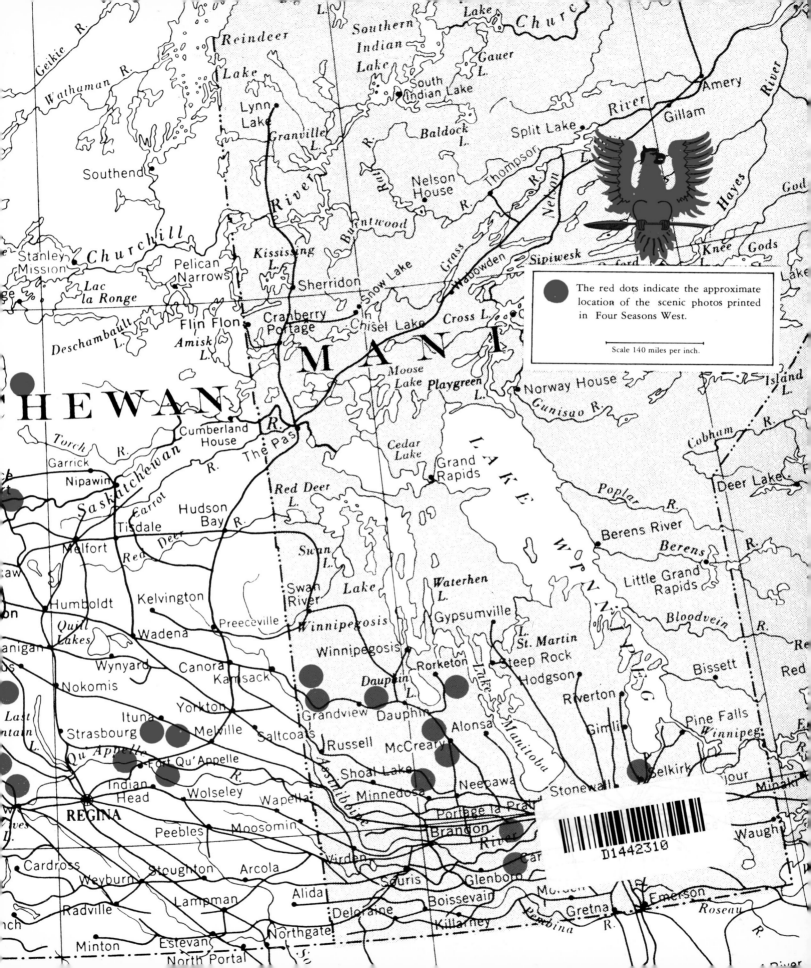

The red dots indicate the approximate location of the scenic photos printed in *Four Seasons West*.

Scale 140 miles per inch.

FOUR
SEASONS
WEST

FOUR SEASONS WEST

A Photographic Odyssey of the Three Prairie Provinces

by

R. H. Macdonald

Western Producer Prairie Books

Saskatoon, Saskatchewan

1975

Copyright © 1975
Western Producer Prairie Books
Saskatoon, Saskatchewan

ISBN 0-919306-55-1

Photo Editor: Doris Macdonald
Book Design: W. Perehudoff
Color separations: General
Graphic Services Ltd., Saskatoon

Printed and bound in Canada
by
Modern Press Ltd.
Saskatoon

To the farmers of Western Canada and their families who, when they work the land, do so in such a way that it adds to Nature's beauty.

With best regards
Rusty macdonald

Four Seasons West

The Oldtimer lifted a hand, curved to fit a plow handle, and pointed toward the sun settling behind distant Cypress Hills. Then he indicated a fold in his own huge spread of land where one scrubby poplar tree and a few chokecherry and saskatoon berry shrubs stood high enough to capture the last beams of light traveling almost parallel to the surface. They stood out in flaming relief from the gathering gloom around them.

When he had "broke" the land years before, he explained, he had left that one clump of shrubs untouched within view of his farmhouse for whatever beauty it would bring.

"You know, I look at that little clump every day. It's never the same — it changes with the seasons and with the light. You've got to get to know the prairie, you've got to spend time on it." After a long pause during which the light faded, he added, "There's beauty on the prairie, you've just got to work a little harder to find it."

★　★　★

The Oldtimer's opinion of the prairie was spoken in the 1940s and his words have echoed over years spent searching for just such beauty. Others before him had striven with the problem of defining the many faceted mystery of the plains and as time and conditions changed so did the overriding impressions. Multitudinous though they are, they appear to fall into four categories.

The early textbook impression — the first impression — was that the West was a land of ice, snow and fur-bearing animals. Original tourists who survived to write about their experiences did little to dispel that view. Among them was William F. Butler who from October 1870 until February 1871 reconnoitred what is now Manitoba, Saskatchewan and Alberta. Two years after his trip from the Red River to the Rocky Mountains and back he wrote a book about his experience and called it **The Great Lone Land.** The title caught the imagination of the civilized world and the first impression stood confirmed.

At the turn of the century the first few tentative forays made by pioneer settlers became virtual waves of immigration. Those who had the time and the inclination wrote home to relatives and friends and the hair-raising tales of labor and hardship under extreme conditions contained in their letters did little to alter the picture left by Captain Butler.

As transportation improved and as wheat, the second product of the west after fur, began reaching hungry markets abroad, a second impression began to take shape. In the boom days that followed the west became known optimistically as a land of opportunity that promised free farms and reward for the strong, the enterprising, the hard working. Just as northern goldfields had produced wealth for some, so the soil of the newly opened territory could be mined to produce fortunes in a golden flow of wheat.

The second impression stood for a time in the public mind and was reinforced as the Canadian West helped feed the allied armies during the First Great War, 1914-1918. Optimism had its high and low points, but the impression held until the 1930s.

As grain markets collapsed and as drought and depression clamped down on the Prairies the third impression came into being. The Canadian West became the dust bowl of the country and photographs of drifting soil and abandoned farmhouses showed it as such to the world. The impression of the Dirty Thirties — of the dreariness of the prairie scene — proved to be a hard one to shake and even now it is vividly remembered by many who experienced it. Indeed, the impression of a deserted land is one not easily erased from the minds of casual visitors who make quick trips along the highways from Winnipeg to Banff or Jasper and certainly not from the minds of those who fly over the vast, monotonous expanse of chequer-boarded terrain twenty thousand feet or more below them.

As the Oldtimer said, there is beauty to be found on the prairie but it takes time and effort to discover it. No doubt there were moments when the early settlers felt just as he did but during an era when "there was never daylight enough or time to do all the chores" the more pressing practical needs commanded attention and left little or no free time in which to set down on paper the esthetic wonders of the new land.

Today the country is settled. Techniques and tools have been developed and they provide plainsmen and plainswomen with a more even footing in their battle with the land and the elements. Many of the basic problems which literally consumed early settlers completely have been solved and their beneficiaries find themselves with more leisure and opportunity to discover and enjoy the unique and unconventional beauty of their surroundings: the unparalleled sunsets, dawns gentle and dawns dramatic, huge skies through which stride unusual and ever-changing cloud formations, clean light affording unrestricted views of the horizon, the many moods of the seasons: spring, summer, fall and winter.

This sense of its beauty is the fourth impression of the prairie. It is the one in which the Oldtimer believed. It is the impression this book is designed to express, especially in the most difficult period — winter.

It has been well over thirty years since the Oldtimer spoke. The photographs that follow are the result of a continuing search during the intervening years for evidence in support of his words. To the extent that they succeed, the fourth impression will have been strengthened — the impression that there is, indeed, beauty in the four seasons west.

ACKNOWLEDGMENTS

Many people made this publication possible including able craftsmen from the paper-making stage through composing, printing, color reproduction and binding. The author is also pleased to acknowledge specifically the help and encouragement of the following:

R. H. D. PHILLIPS, Editor and Publisher of **The Western Producer** who first suggested and then persisted in seeing that **Four Seasons West** became a fact.

THE CANADA COUNCIL whose Block Grant program, designed to assist the publishing of Canadian books in Canada, made it possible to include many more full color reproductions than would have been possible otherwise.

THE PHOTO EDITOR Doris Macdonald, who over the years has sorted, selected, titled, filed and thus rescued color transparencies from oblivion and who has been a helpful and welcome companion on many of the trips on which these photos were taken.

THE DESIGNER W. Perehudoff, who, a creative artist of international repute himself, loaned his considerable abilities in order to make this book, from front to back, the graceful publication it is.

11

Spring

Spring Break-Up, Jackfish Lake, Sask.   17

Early Spring, Minnedosa District, Man.   18

Last of the Snow, Central Saskatchewan   19

Prairie Spring Sunset, Tuxford, Sask.   20

Spring Reflections, Hamlin, Sask.   22

Outcropping in Rosebud River Valley, near Strathmore, Alta.   23

Spring Reflections, Northern Saskatchewan Marshlands   24

Northern Marsh Study, Saskatchewan   25

Sunrise, Roblin, Man.   26

Spring Reflections, Battleford District, Sask.   27

Spring Seeding, near Herschel, Sask.   28

Reflections on Tributary, Duck Lake, Sask.   30

Deserted Homestead, Colonsay District, Sask.   31

Bush-Lined Slough in Spring, near Penzance, Sask.   32

Spring

The prairie spring can be a month early or a month late but, more often than not, its arrival will be sudden. As if by the wave of a magic wand, once-gray winter cloudbanks turn into a thousand white cumulous balls of fluff against a robin egg blue background. Warm westerly winds sweat water out of snow; potholes, sloughs, lakes and muskeg fill with crystal clear pools, reflecting the sky as if mirrors had been sprinkled over the land. Spring showers follow closely leaving paddy green leaves clean, fresh and dotted with fairy crystal balls. There is birdsong; farmers warm up their machines — suddenly the countryside has turned pliant and green.

adrops on new leaves taken on an Alberta farm shelterbelt.

Spring Break-Up, Jackfish Lake, Sask.

Early Spring, Minnedosa District, Man.

(overleaf) Prairie Spring Sunset, Tuxford, Sask.

Outcroppings in Rosebud River Valley, near Strathmore, Alta.

ng Reflections, Hamlin, Sask.

Northern Marsh Study, Saskatchewan

Sunrise, Roblin, Man.

Spring Reflections, Battleford District, Sask.

27

(*overleaf*) Spring Seeding, near Herschel, Sask.

Reflections on Tributary, Duck Lake, Sask.

30

Deserted Homestead, Colonsay District, Sask.

Bush-Lined Slough in Spring, near Penzance, Sask.

Summer

Sun-Dappled Poplar Grove, Northern Sask.   37

Farmstead and Big Sky, near Sibbald, Alta.   38

Sunset over Clear Lake, Man.   39

Sunrays, Delisle, Sask.   40

Pastoral Scene After Storm, Saskatoon district, Sask.   42

Late Summer Colors west of Morrin, Alta.   43

Quiet Reflections in Badlands, Red Deer River, Alta.   44

Sunset, Waskesiu Lake, Sask.   45

Lake of the Prairies Reflections, Valleyview, Man.   46

Golden Rape Fields, Bankend, Sask.   47

Dramatic Sunset, Prince Albert National Park, Sask.   48

Wheat Swath, Bow Island district of Southern Alberta   49

Saskatchewan River and Rainstorm, Batoche, Sask.   50

Early Manitoba Farmstead, Carberry, Man.   51

Dramatic Storm Clouds Over Farmstead, Warman, Sask.   52

Moody Afterglow, Hanging Hart Lakes, Sask.   53

Storm Scene — Prairie Town, Tessier District, Sask.   54

Sunset on Northern Saskatchewan Lake   56

Summer

Prairie summer is the time of the sky. Small morning clouds by late afternoon become towering billows reaching tens of thousands of feet in the air; moist clouds the tone of old silver combine to draw behind them veils of welcome rain over the thirsty land; crops turn green, bloom and ripen, each with its own most attractive stage. In lower latitudes wheat will often ripen before summer's end and then the crop is cut and placed on the land in golden ropes as thick as the braids of a sun-kissed prairie girl.

y Meadow, Manitoba

Sun-Dappled Poplar Grove, Northern Sas

36

Farmstead and Big Sky, near Sibbald, Alta.

Sunset over Clear Lake, Man.

(*overleaf*) Sunrays, Delisle, Sask.

Pastoral Scene After Storm, Saskatoon District, Sask.

Late Summer Colors, West of Morrin, Alt

Quiet Reflections in Badlands, Red Deer River, Alta.

Sunset, Waskesiu Lake, Sask.

Lake of the Prairies Reflections, Valleyview, Man.

Golden Rape Fields, Bankend, S

Dramatic Sunset, Prince Albert National Park, Sask.

Wheat Swath — Bow Island district of Southern Alberta.

Saskatchewan River and Rainstorm, Batoche, Sask.

Early Manitoba Farmstead, Carberry, Man.

Moody Afterglow, Hanging Hart Lakes, Sask.

atic Storm Clouds Over Farmstead, Warman, Sask.

(overleaf) Storm Scene — Prairie Town, Tessier District, Sask.

Fall

Prairie Harvest 61

Fall Colors on bank of South Saskatchewan River near Rosthern, Sask. 62

Sun Rays and Lone Tree, near Kincorth, Sask. 63

Combining, Erickson, Man. 64

Sunset on Montreal Lake, Northern Saskatchewan 65

Color in the Coulee, Saskatchewan Landing, Sask. 66

Harvest scene, Somerset District, Man. 67

Distant Scenic, Pearce, Alta. 68

Fall Color in the Saskatchewan River Valley, Sask. 69

Moody Skies over 'The Big Country', near Cowley, Alta. 70

Off to School, south of Prince Albert, Sask. 72

Roadside Scene in Harvest, near Dauphin, Man. 73

Four Combines at Work, Starbuck District, Man. 74

Swathing Oats, near Three Hills, Alta. 75

Qu'Appelle Valley Scenic, Southern Saskatchewan 76

Harvesting, north of Drumheller, Alta. 78

Cottonwoods in Fall, near Maple Creek, Sask. 79

Old Man River Valley Scenic, Brocket, Alta. 80

Sunset on Northern Saskatchewan Lake

Fall

In the fall the prairie turns gold and men on giant machines travel up and down the fields gathering treasure. Sky and land challenge one another in a battle of color and drama. Eye-catching scenes await the observer: striking patterns reaching toward blue hills on the far horizon; the subtle colors and tones in one of the prairie's sudden valleys; country grain elevators, tall in the distance, as someone has already said, stitching land and sky together like slender staples.

Oat stooks in Qu'Appelle Valley.

Kodak International Color Competition "Special Award for Photographic Excellence" New York World's Fair 1964-1965   Prairie Harvest

Fall colors on bank of South Saskatchewan River near Rosthern, Sask.

Sun Rays and Lone Tree, near Kincorth, Sask.

Combining, Erickson, Man.

Sunset on Montreal Lake, Northern Saskatchewan

Color in the Coulee, Saskatchewan Landing, Sask.

Harvest scene, Somerset District, Man.

Distant Scenic, Pearce, Alta.

Fall color in the Saskatchewan River Valley, Sask.

(overleaf) Moody Skies over 'The Big Country', near Cowley, Alta.

Off to School, south of Prince Albert, Sask.

Roadside Scene in Harvest, near Dauphin, Man.

Four Combines at Work, Starbuck District, Man.

Swathing Oats, near Three Hills, Alta.

(overleaf) Qu'Appelle Valley Scenic, Southern Saskatchewan

Harvesting, north of Drumheller, Alta.

Cottonwoods in Fall, near Maple Creek, Sask. ▶

Winter

Hoar Frost and Mist, Saskatoon, Sask.   85

Indian Ponies, Kananaskis District, Alta.   86

Dawn, Ridpath, Sask.   87

Prairie Town in Winter, Dysart, Sask.   88

Fields of Slipper Satin Snow, Alsask-Hanna District, Alta.   90

Frosty Winter Dawn, Kinley, Sask.   91

Misty Morn, near Moose Jaw, Sask.   92

Hoar Frost Scenic, Ranfurly District, Alta.   93

Winter Prairie Dawn, Meacham, Sask.   94

Winter Blossomtime, near Prince Albert, Sask.   95

Farmstead near Colonsay, Sask.   96

Late Winter Afternoon, near Red Deer Hill, Sask.   98

Winter Dawn, D'Arcy, Sask.   99

Prairie Trail in Late Afternoon, Prongua, Sask.   100

Cows Homeward Bound, Cochrane District, Alta.   101

Dawn Over Laura, Sask.   102

Winter Moonrise, Blackfoot, Alta.   104

Prairie in Deep Freeze, Elstow District, Sask.   105

Old St. Andrew's on the Red River, near Lockport, Man.   106

Mt. Agassiz Ski Resort, Riding Mountain National Park, Man.   107

Sunrise and Frosted Bluff, Blucher District, Sask.   108

Winter Field Study, Central Saskatchewan.   109

Frosty Sunrise, near Ellerslie, Alta.   110

Horses in Winter Pasture, Delia District, Alta.   111

Winter Pasture and Late Afternoon — Looking to Minburn, Alta.   112

d Man River Valley Scenic, Brocket, Alta.

Winter

For years the prairie winter was deemed the enemy of man but
recently developed insulating fabrics and technology have
changed all that and have brought the discovery of new
beauty with them. And beauty there is: thick ropes of frost
turning the commonplace into a fairy wonderland; an icy dawn
dressed in warm colors; slanted early evening light bringing
a touch of comfort to a lonely scene; snow, snow — whether the
soft protected pillows in parkland forest, wind-polished
slipper satin snow of the open prairie, or wind-whipped
streams steaming like smoke over the flat blacktopped highway.
As if to compensate man, Nature saves some of her most
captivating moods for those hardy enough to brave the outdoors
in thirty or forty-below zero weather.

ind-sculptured snow on the Regina Plains.

Hoar Frost and Mist, Saskatoon, Sask.

Indian Ponies, Kananaskis District, Alta.

Dawn, Ridpath, Sask.

(overleaf)   Prairie Town in Winter, Dysart, Sask.

Fields of Slipper Satin Snow, Alsask-Hanna District, Alta.

90

Hoar Frost Scenic, Ranfurly District, Alta.

Winter Prairie Dawn, Meacham, Sask.

Winter Blossomtime, near Prince Albert, S

(overleaf) Farmstead near Colonsay, Sask.

Late Winter Afternoon, near Red Deer Hill, Sask.

Winter Dawn, D'Arcy, Sask.

(overleaf) Prairie Trail in Late Afternoon, Prongua, Sask.
(overleaf) Cows Homeward Bound, Cochrane District, Alta.

Winter Moonrise, Blackfoot, Alta.

Prairie in Deep Freeze, Elstow District, S

(overleaf) ◄ Dawn Over Laura, Sask.

Old St. Andrew's on the Red River, near Lockport, Man.

Mt. Agassiz Ski Resort, Riding Mountain National Park, Man.

Sunrise and Frosted Bluff, Blucher District, Sask.

108

Winter Field Study, Central Saskatchewan.

Frosty Sunrise, near Ellerslie, Alta.

Horses in Winter Pasture, Delia District, Alta.

Winter Pasture and Late Afternoon — Looking to Minburn, Alta.